AFFINITIES

Developing Intimacy with God Companion Journal

By Christine Joy

Altered Pages Bible Studies enrich biblical exploration, blending in-depth study with practical applications and effective visual journaling tools. Dive into Scripture's timeless truths, apply them to your life, and unleash your creativity!

For the Affinities study and more information, visit:
www.christinejoystudies.com

© Copyright 2024 CJB Designs LLC and licensors.
Scripture quotations identified as ESV are from the *English Standard Version*. Copyright 2001 by Crossway, a publishing ministry of Good News Publishers. All rights reserved.

Contents

Welcome……………………………………………………………………………………3

Chapter 1
Your Best Life………………………………………………………………………7

Chapter 2
Ultimate Power……………………………………………………………………13

Chapter 3
You Are Loved……………………………………………………………………23

Chapter 4
You Are Valued……………………………………………………………………41

Chapter 5
You Belong………………………………………………………………………57

Chapter 6
Embracing the Mystery……………………………………………………………73

Trinity Verses………………………………………………………………………78

Welcome to Your Journal!

I'm so glad you're here- ready to explore, reflect, and grow in your relationship with God.

This journal is your personal space to engage deeper with the themes of *Affinities* in your own words and your own way. We'll unpack exactly what an affinity is as we begin to develop this deep longing for the Most High God through journaling.

Sometimes, we struggle to connect with an invisible God. As the study explores connectedness and discovers the relational, emotional, and communal aspects of nearness to God, this journal is meant to help you process what you're learning. As you respond to prompts and add your doodles, you'll be invited to let go of control, rest in the presence of God, and find joy in the fellowship of the Holy Trinity.

This space is for your insights, doubts, your questions, and your worship. It's not about perfection, it's about being in the presence of God. Use this journal alongside the study, whether on your own or in a group. Slow down and listen to what God is doing in your heart.

Use whatever tools you enjoy- pens, pencils, markers, or paint- and let your creativity be a form of intimacy with the Lord. Think of it as bullet journaling meets Bible study. Use the examples at the end of each chapter of the study for inspiration.

Let this be your sacred space. As we study together, no judgment- imperfect people are welcome here! – Christine Joy

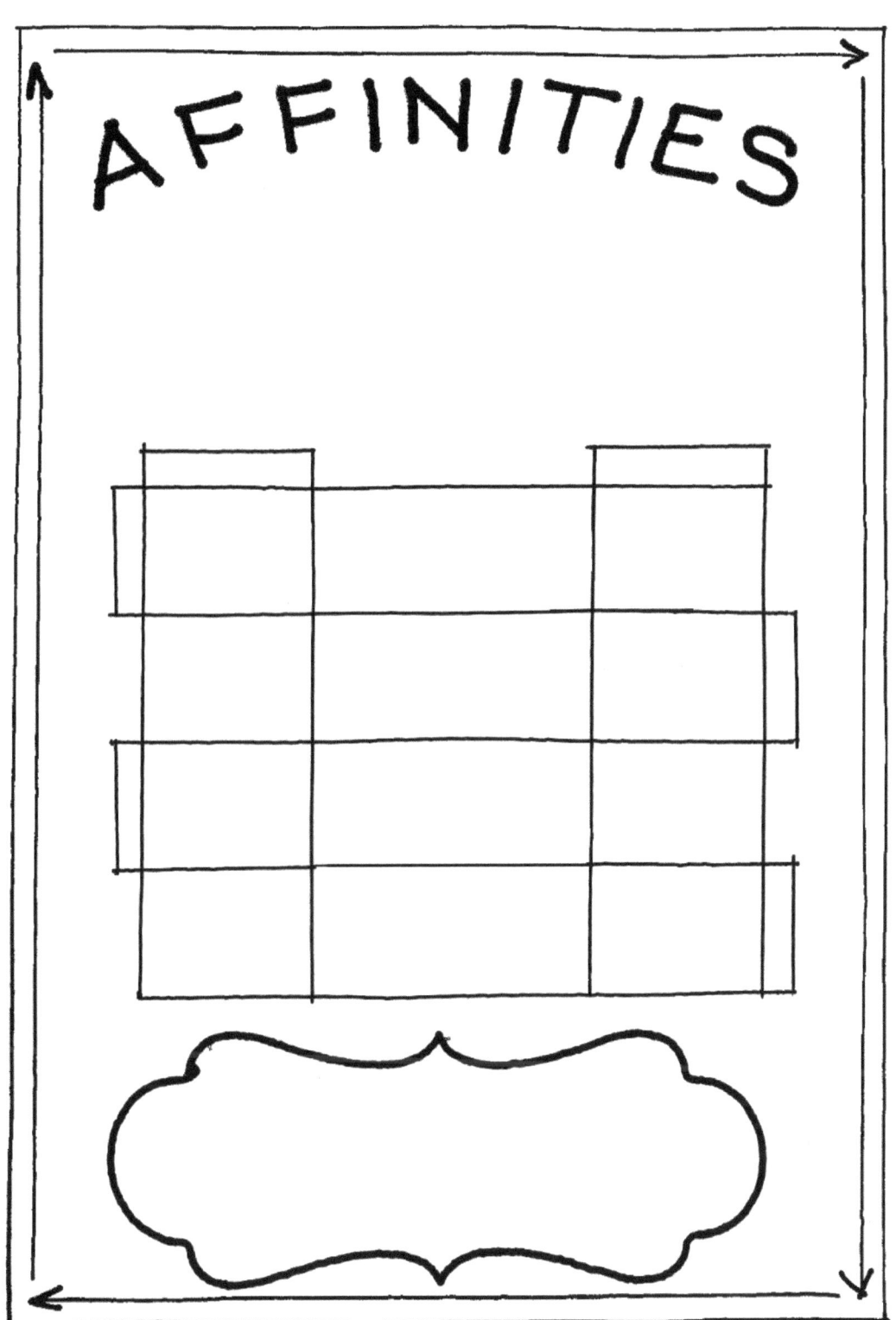

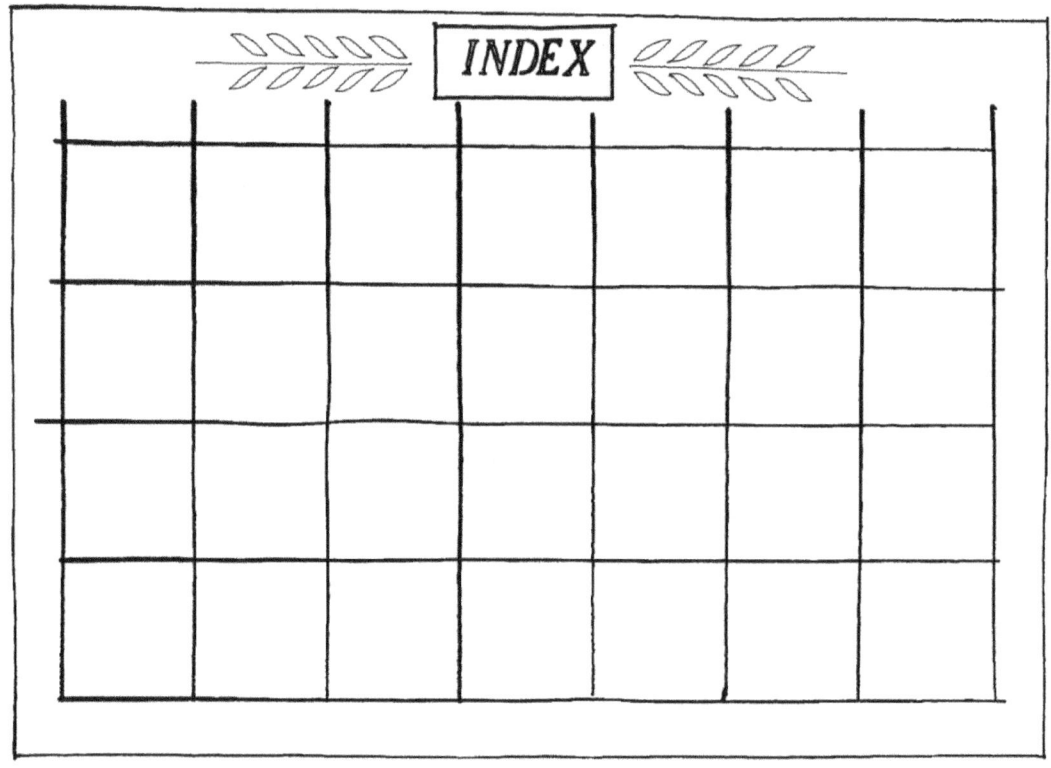

Chapter One:

Your Best Life

> We will explore ways to cultivate a rapport with each person of the Trinity that is exciting and endearing, along with overcoming common difficulties that can get in the way. All of this is to live our best God-given lives.

_____
_____
_____
_____
_____
_____
_____
_____
_____

Affinity for God

Obstacles

Strategies

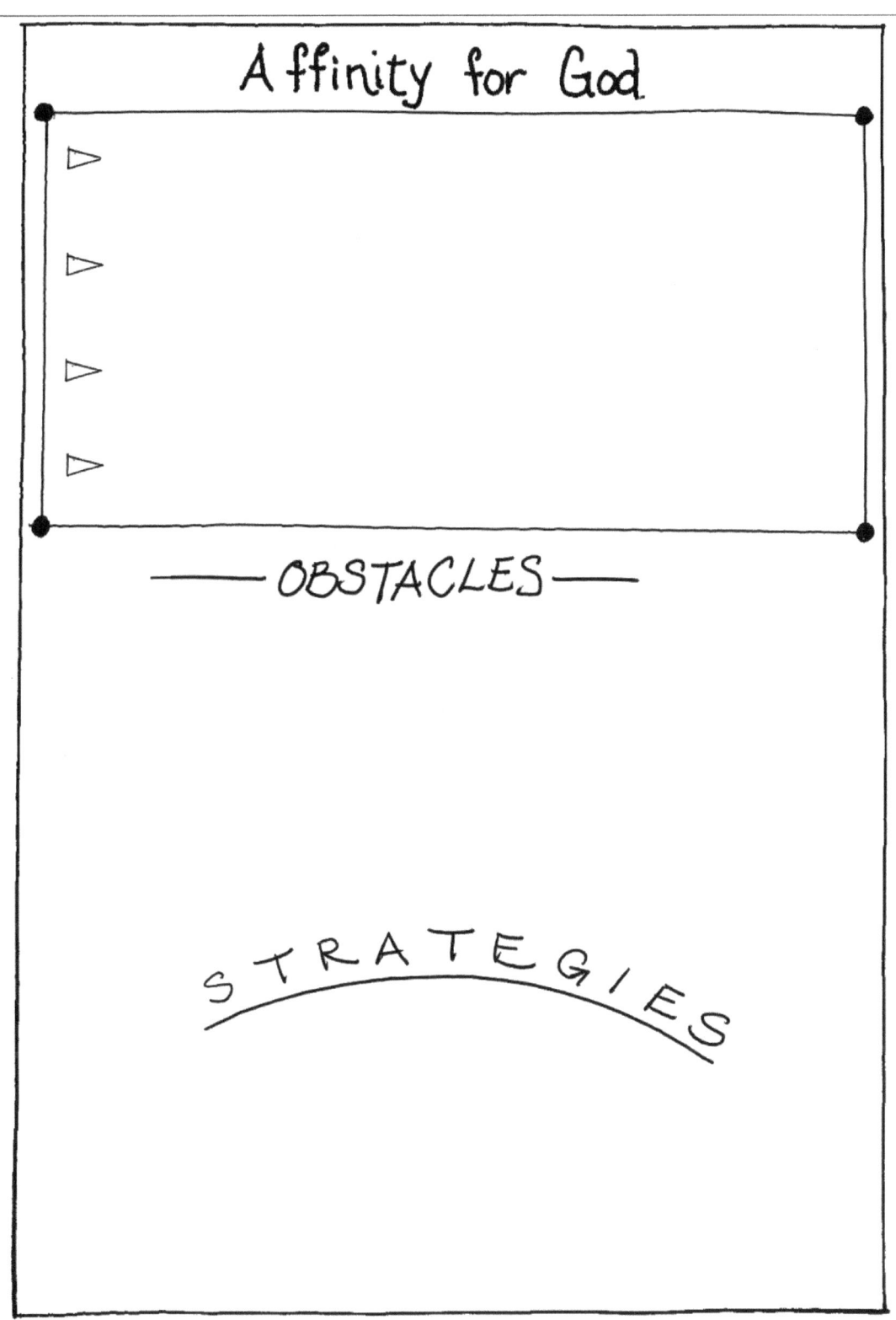

Draw near to God and He will draw near to you – James 4:8

Challenges:

Chapter Two:
Ultimate Power

> I am not my own.
>
> I belong to the One True God!

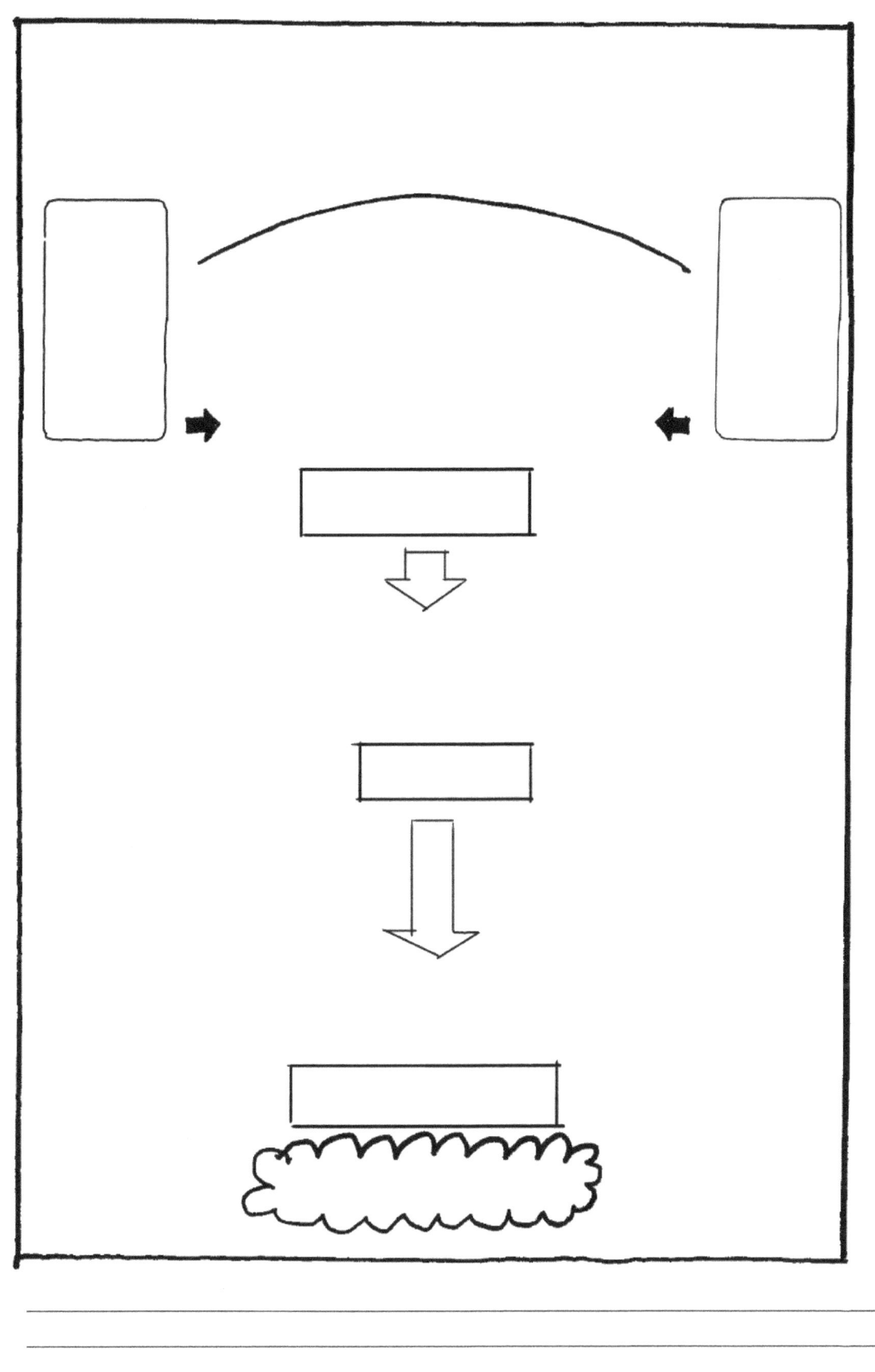

SECTION ONE: GOD ALL- MIGHTY

Attributes of Glory

God is:	Verse(s)
1. _____	John 4:24; 1 Timothy 1:17
2. _____	Psalm 90:1-2; 1 Timothy 1:17
3. _____	Psalm 102:27; Malachi 3:6; James 1:17
4. _____	Genesis 17:1; Matthew 19:26
5. _____	John 21:17; Psalm 139:1-2
6. _____	Jeremiah 23:24; Proverbs 15:3
7. _____	Leviticus 19:2; Isaiah 6:3

_____
_____
_____
_____
_____
_____
_____
_____

Attributes of Righteousness

God is:	Verse(s)
1. _____	Deuteronomy 32:4; Romans 11:33
2. _____	Psalm 36:5b; 2 Timothy 2:13; Jeremiah 3:12
3. _____	Numbers 14:18a; Psalm 103:8
4. _____	Psalm 118:1; Psalm 145:9
5. _____	Psalm 145:9; Exodus 22:27; 2 Samuel 24:14
6. _____	Exodus 34:6-7; Psalm 86:5
7. _____	Psalm 36:5a; John 3:16; 1 John 4:8

_____
_____
_____
_____
_____
_____
_____
_____

SECTION TWO: FREEDOM!

Confession + Absolution

_____
_____
_____
_____
_____
_____
_____
_____

1 John 1:8-9 *If we say we have no sin, we deceive ourselves, and the truth is not in us. If we confess our sins, he is faithful and just to forgive us our sins and to cleanse us from all unrighteousness.*

John 8:36 *So if the Son sets you free, you will be free indeed.*

Challenges:

Chapter Three:
You Are Loved

> To build a relationship with our Heavenly Dad, we must actively and firmly trust Him. We trust that He loves and cherishes us; we trust that He knows what's best for us; and we trust Him to lead us throughout our life.

SECTION ONE: THE TRIUNE GOD

Genesis 1:1-2 *In the beginning, God created the heavens and the earth. ² The earth was without form and void, and darkness was over the face of the deep. And the Spirit of God was hovering over the face of the waters.*

John 1:1-3, 14 *In the beginning was the Word, and the Word was with God, and the Word was God. ² He was in the beginning with God. ³ All things were made through him, and without him was not any thing made that was made.*
    ¹⁴And the Word became flesh and dwelt among us, and we have seen his glory, glory as of the only Son from the Father, full of grace and truth.

I Believe

THE APOSTLES CREED

I believe in God, the Father Almighty, Maker of heaven and earth.

And in Jesus Christ, His only Son, our Lord, who was conceived by the Holy Spirit, born of the virgin Mary, suffered under Pontius Pilate, was crucified, died and was buried. He descended into hell. The third day He rose again from the dead. He ascended into heaven and sits at the right hand of God the Father Almighty. From thence He will come to judge the living and the dead.

I believe in the Holy Spirit, the holy Christian Church, the communion of saints, the forgiveness of sins, the resurrection of the body, and the life everlasting.
Amen.

SECTION TWO: GOD THE FATHER

1 John 3:1a *See what kind of love the Father has given to us, that we should be called children of God; and so we are.*

_____
_____
_____
_____
_____
_____
_____
_____
_____
_____
_____
_____
_____

THE APOSTLES CREED

I believe in God the Father Almighty, Maker of heaven and earth.

_____
_____
_____
_____
_____
_____
_____
_____
_____
_____
_____
_____

Trinity Sightings
(at end of journal)

	Your thoughts
1	
2	
3	
4	
5	
6	
7	
8	
9	
10	
11	
12	
13	
14	
15	
16	

_____
_____
_____
_____
_____

SECTION THREE: BONDING WITH THE FATHER

TRUST:

1) Submit my will to His

2) Want what the Father wants

3) Spend time with Him in prayer

Challenges:

Chapter Four:

You Are Valued

> I will fear no evil, because Jesus is with me.

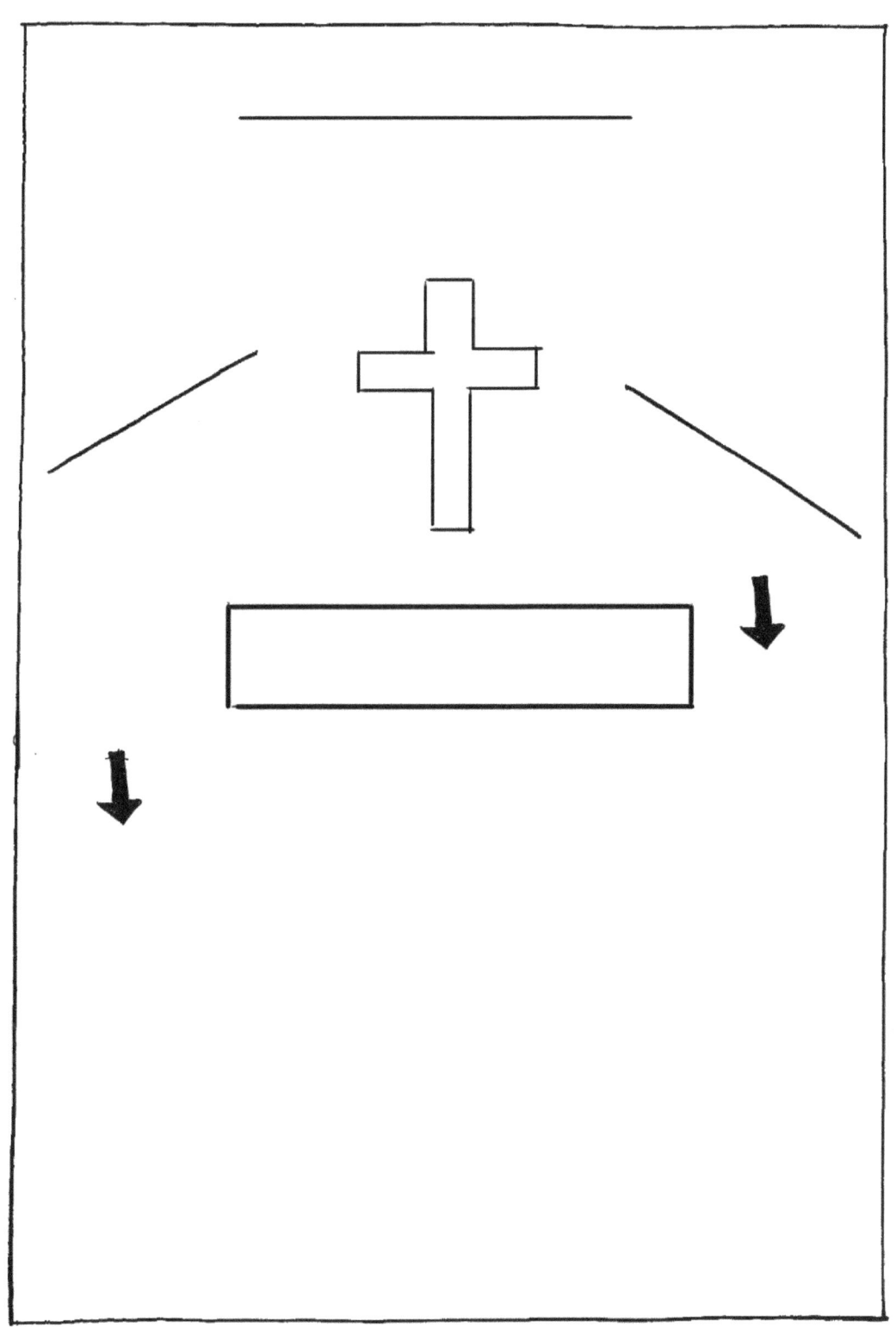

Apostles Creed

And in Jesus Christ, His only Son, our Lord
Who was conceived by the Holy Spirit, born of the virgin Mary,
Suffered under Pontius Pilate, was crucified, died and was buried.
He descended into hell.
The third day He rose again from the dead.
He ascended into heaven and sits at the right hand of God the Father Almighty.
From thence He will come to judge the living and the dead.

SECTION ONE: GOD AND MAN

TRUE GOD

_____
_____
_____
_____
_____
_____
_____
_____

TRUE MAN

_____
_____
_____
_____
_____
_____
_____
_____

SECTION TWO: DELIVERANCE!

TRINITY VERSES:

SECTION THREE:
MY KING, MY SHEPHERD, MY FRIEND, MY JESUS

Psalm 23

- The Lord is my shepherd; I shall not want, for you are with me.
- You make me lie down in green pastures, for you are with me.
- You lead me beside still waters, for you are with me.
- You restore my soul, for you are with me.
- You lead me in paths of righteousness for your name's sake, for you are with me.
- Even though I walk through the valley of the shadow of death, I will fear no evil, for you are with me.
- Your rod and your staff, they comfort me, for you are with me.
- You prepare a table before me in the presence of my enemies, for you are with me.
- You anoint my head with oil, my cup overflows, for you are with me.
- Surely goodness and mercy shall follow me all the days of my life, for you are with me.
- And I shall dwell in the house of the LORD forever, for you are with me.

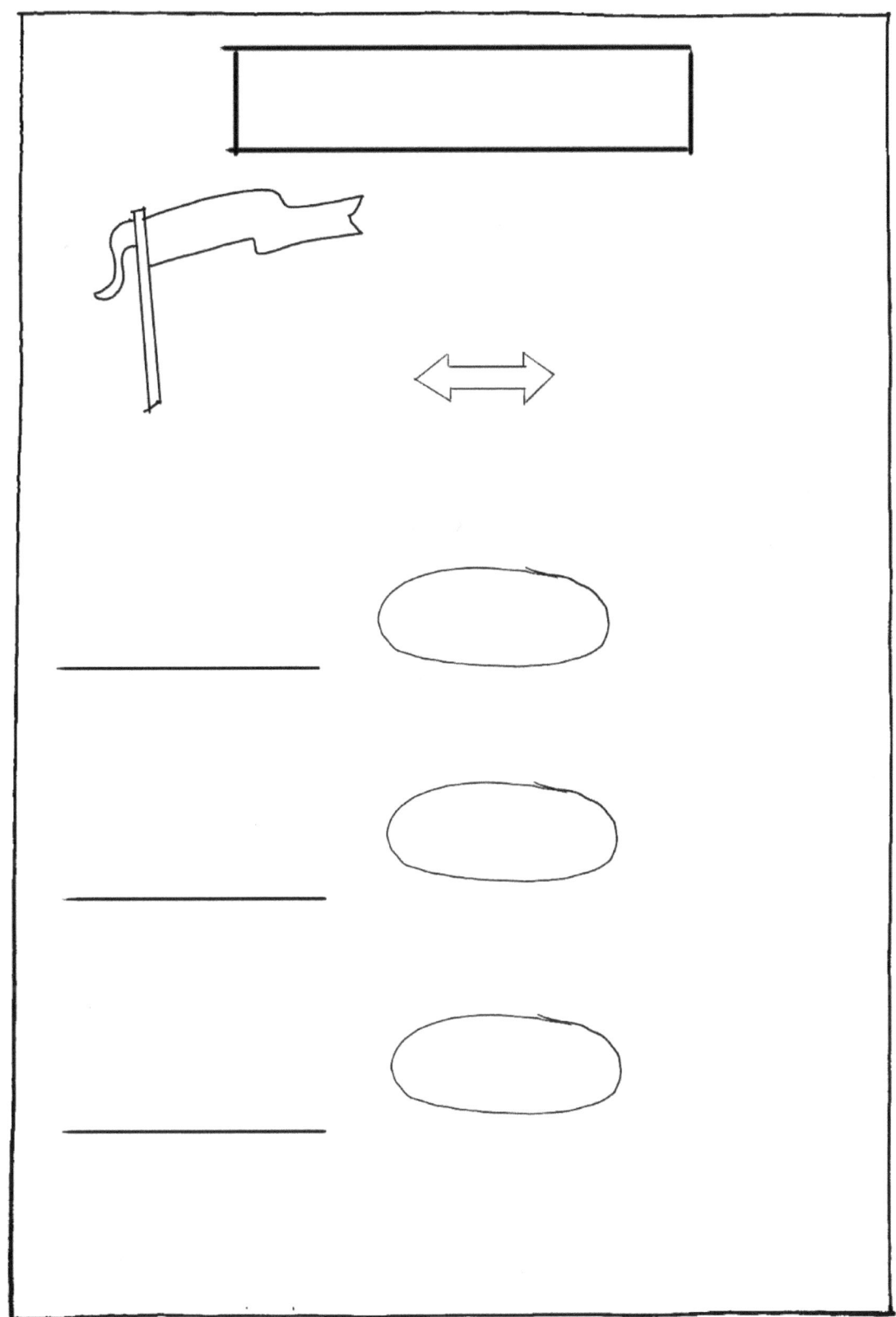

Challenges:

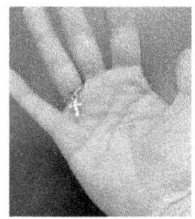

Chapter Five:
You Belong

> We are never meant to be a follower of Christ on our own. We are to be part of a Christian community.

The Spirit of God

	Trinity Verses
1	
2	
3	
4	
5	
6	
7	
8	
9	
10	
11	
12	
13	
14	
15	
16	

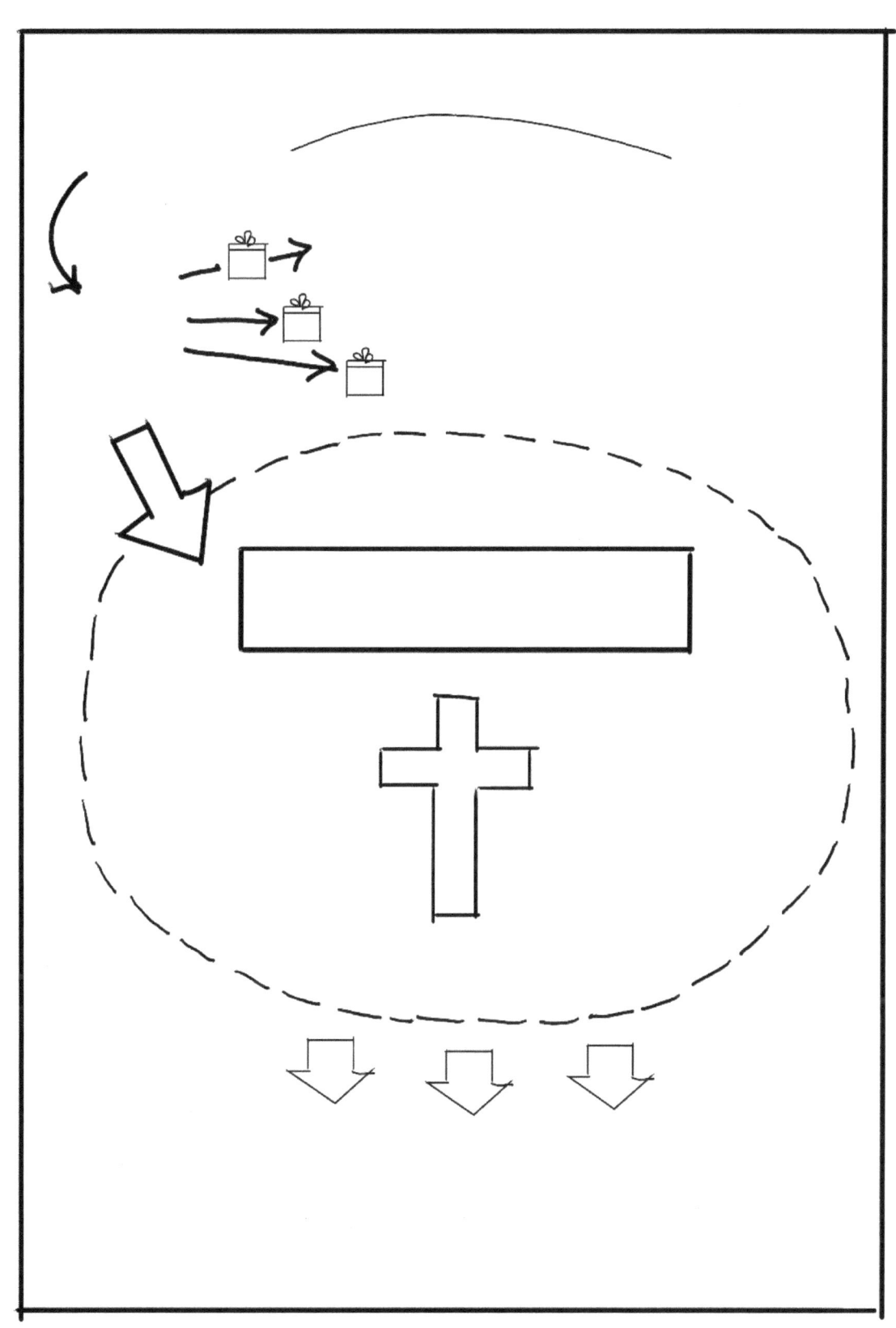

SECTION ONE: THE SANCTIFIER

THE APOSTLES CREED

I believe in the Holy Spirit, the holy Christian church, the communion of saints, the forgiveness of sins, the resurrection of the body, and the life everlasting.

2 Corinthians 3:18 *And we all, with unveiled face, beholding the glory of the Lord, are being transformed into the same image from one degree of glory to another. For this comes from the Lord who is the Spirit.*

FORGIVENESS

Job 19:25-27 *For I know that my Redeemer lives, and at the last he will stand upon the earth. ²⁶ And after my skin has been thus destroyed, yet in my flesh I shall see God, ²⁷ whom I shall see for myself, and my eyes shall behold, and not another.*

SECTION TWO: FRUIT!

Spiritual Gifts

Challenges:

Chapter Six:

Embracing the Mystery

> My Father saves me through Jesus Christ by the power of the Holy Spirit

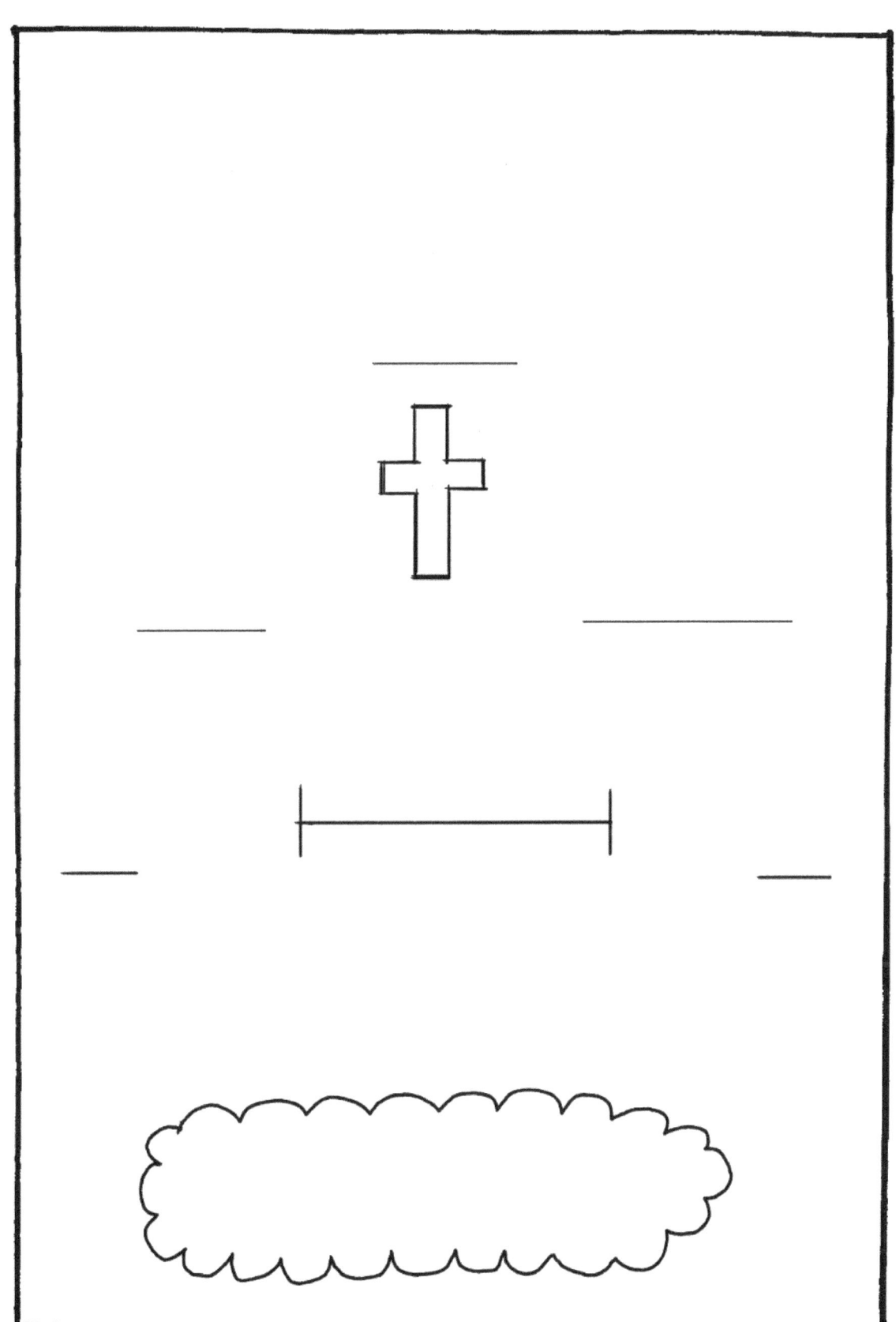

Psalm 16:11 *You make known to me the path of life; in your presence there is fullness of joy; at your right hand are pleasures forevermore.*

TRINITY SIGHTINGS

1. Matthew 3:16-17: *And when Jesus was baptized, immediately he went up from the water, and behold, the heavens were opened to him, and he saw the Spirit of God descending like a dove and coming to rest on him; [17] and behold, a voice from heaven said, "This is my beloved Son, with whom I am well pleased. (Luke 3:21-22; Mark 1:9-11)*

2. Matthew 28:19: *Go therefore and make disciples of all nations, baptizing them in the name of the Father and of the Son and of the Holy Spirit,*

3. John 14:16-17: *And I will ask the Father, and he will give you another Helper, to be with you forever, [17] even the Spirit of truth, whom the world cannot receive, because it neither sees him nor knows him. You know him, for he dwells with you and will be in you.*

4. John 15:26: *"But when the Helper comes, whom I will send to you from the Father, the Spirit of truth, who proceeds from the Father, he will bear witness about me.*

5. Acts 1:4-5: *And while staying with them he ordered them not to depart from Jerusalem, but to wait for the promise of the Father, which, he said, "you heard from me; [5] for John baptized with water, but you will be baptized with the Holy Spirit not many days from now."*

6. Acts 2:33: *Being therefore exalted at the right hand of God, and having received from the Father the promise of the Holy Spirit, he has poured out this that you yourselves are seeing and hearing.*

7. Romans 14:17-18: *For the kingdom of God is not a matter of eating and drinking but of righteousness and peace and joy in the Holy Spirit. [18] Whoever thus serves Christ is acceptable to God and approved by men.*

8. 1 Corinthians 12:4-6: *Now there are varieties of gifts, but the same Spirit; [5] and there are varieties of service, but the same Lord; [6] and there are varieties of activities, but it is the same God who empowers them all in everyone.*

9. 2 Corinthians 1:21-22: *And it is God who establishes us with you in Christ, and has anointed us, ²² and who has also put his seal on us and given us his Spirit in our hearts as a guarantee.*

10. 2 Corinthians 13:14: *The grace of the Lord Jesus Christ and the love of God and the fellowship of the Holy Spirit be with you all.*

11. Galatians 4:6: *And because you are sons, God has sent the Spirit of his Son into our hearts, crying, "Abba! Father!"*

12. Ephesians 1:17: *that the God of our Lord Jesus Christ, the Father of glory, may give you the Spirit of wisdom and of revelation in the knowledge of him,*

13. Ephesians 2:17-18: *And he came and preached peace to you who were far off and peace to those who were near. ¹⁸ For through him we both have access in one Spirit to the Father*

14. Ephesians 4:4-6: *There is one body and one Spirit—just as you were called to the one hope that belongs to your call— ⁵ one Lord, one faith, one baptism, ⁶ one God and Father of all, who is over all and through all and in all.*

15. 1 Peter 1:1-2: *Peter, an apostle of Jesus Christ, To those who are elect exiles of the Dispersion in Pontus, Galatia, Cappadocia, Asia, and Bithynia, ² according to the foreknowledge of God the Father, in the sanctification of the Spirit, for obedience to Jesus Christ and for sprinkling with his blood: May grace and peace be multiplied to you*

16. Jude 20-21: *But you, beloved, building yourselves up in your most holy faith and praying in the Holy Spirit, ²¹ keep yourselves in the love of God, waiting for the mercy of our Lord Jesus Christ that leads to eternal life.*

www.ingramcontent.com/pod-product-compliance
Lightning Source LLC
Chambersburg PA
CBHW042359070526
44585CB00029B/2993